The Ultimate *Giraffe* Book for Kids

www.bellanovabooks.com

Copyright © 2026 by Jenny Kellett

All rights reserved. No part of this book may be reproduced in any form by any electronic or mechanical means including photocopying, recording, or information storage and retrieval without permission in writing from the author.

Imprint: Bellanova Books
ISBN: 978-619-264-069-9

CONTENTS

Introduction	4
Giraffe Species	6
Northern Giraffe	8
Reticulated Giraffe	10
Masai Giraffe	12
Southern Giraffe	14
Giraffe Facts	16
Giraffe Quiz	78
Quiz Answers	83
Word Search Puzzle	84
Solution	86
Sources	87

INTRODUCTION

It's hard not to love giraffes! They're peculiar, cute, and funny. But how much do you really know about your favorite tall friend?

In this book, you will learn over 100 amazing new things about giraffes—from their eating habits to their unusual way of giving birth. And then you'll have a chance to test your newfound knowledge! You'll be a giraffe expert in no time.

Are you ready? *Let's go!*

GIRAFFE SPECIES

The number of giraffe species is a hot topic among scientists! There is an ongoing debate about how many there are. However, there are currently four officially recognized species:

- **Northern giraffe** (*Giraffa camelopardalis*)
- **Reticulated giraffe** (*Giraffa reticulata*)
- **Masai giraffe** (*Giraffa tippelskirchi*)
- **Southern giraffe** (*Giraffa giraffa*)

Let's take a closer look to see the differences!

A Rothschild's giraffe.
© Bernard Dupont

Northern Giraffe
(Giraffa camelopardalis)

The northern giraffe, also known as the Sahara giraffe, is a species of giraffe found in several countries in Africa, including Chad, Mali, Niger, and Sudan. There are four subspecies of the northern giraffe: the Kordofan giraffe, the Nubian giraffe, the Rothschild's giraffe, and the West African giraffe.

The northern giraffe is known for its distinctive coat pattern, which features large, irregularly-shaped brown patches separated by thin white lines.

© Roland H

Northern giraffes have longer necks compared to other species of giraffes, and they can reach a height of up to 5.5 meters (18 feet).

Unfortunately, the northern giraffe is considered to be a threatened species, with a declining population due to habitat loss, civil unrest, and illegal hunting.

THE ULTIMATE GIRAFFE BOOK

The reticulated giraffe, also known as the **Somali giraffe**, is a species of giraffe found in several countries in East Africa, including Kenya, Somalia, South Sudan, and Ethiopia. It is one of the most commonly seen in zoos around the world.

The reticulated giraffe is known for its distinctive coat pattern, which features a network of white lines that form a reticulated, or net-like, pattern on a dark background.

A young reticulated giraffe.

Reticulated giraffes are medium-sized giraffes, reaching a height of up to 5.5 meters (18 feet). They are herbivores and feed mainly on leaves, flowers, and fruits from trees and bushes.

The reticulated giraffe is considered to be a vulnerable species. There are around 8,500 living in the wild.

The Masai giraffe, also known as the **Kilimanjaro giraffe**, is a species of giraffe found in several countries in East Africa, including Kenya, Tanzania, and Zambia. There are two subspecies of Masai giraffe: the Masai giraffe and the Thornicroft's giraffe.

The Masai giraffe (subspecies) has a diverse range of coat patterns, including rounded and smooth spots to oval and jagged. There are around 32,550 living in the wild. The Thornicroft's giraffe has spots that are almost star-shaped. There are less than 500 left in the wild.

A Masai giraffe.

Southern Giraffe
(*Giraffa giraffa*)

The Southern Giraffe is found in southern Africa in countries such as South Africa, Zambia and Namibia. There are two subspecies: the **Angolan giraffe** and the **South African giraffe**.

The Angolan giraffe has large brown, blotchy spots across all of its body except the upper part of the face. They also have a white ear patch. There are around 13,000 living in the wild.

The South African giraffe has dark, rounded patches on a tawny background. There are around 31,500 living in the wild.

South African giraffes. © Luca Galuzzi - www.galuzzi.it

GIRAFFE FACTS

Giraffes are the tallest mammals on Earth. Their legs alone are around 6 ft (183 cm) high!

...

Adult giraffes stand 14.1–18.7 ft (4.3–5.7 m) tall. Males are taller and heavier than females.

...

Those long legs are put to good use! While they're no match for a cheetah, giraffes can run at speeds of up to 35 mph (56.3 km/h) over short distances.

THE ULTIMATE GIRAFFE BOOK

Giraffes only drink every few days. Most of their water comes from the food that they eat.

• • •

Giraffes are famous for their long necks, but they're still not long enough to reach the ground! When drinking water, giraffes must awkwardly spread their legs sideways, or kneel down, to be able to get low enough.

• • •

Despite such long necks, giraffes have the same amount of vertebrae as humans—seven. However, each vertebra can be up to 10 inches (25.4 cm) wide.

A curious giraffe in South Africa.

A giraffe's neck can be up to 2–2.4 m (6.6–7.9 ft) in length. However, they have relatively short bodies, so most of their height comes from their legs and neck.

Giraffes spend most of their lives standing up. They even give birth standing up!

• • •

Baby giraffes are called **calves**.

• • •

Female calves are called **cows**, while males are called **bulls**.

• • •

When a giraffe gives birth, her calf falls straight to the ground. The fall can be from as high as 5 feet (1.5 m)!

A giraffe in its natural savannah habitat in sub-saharan Africa.

When calves are born, they are already taller than most humans — around 6 feet (1.8 m).

• • •

Despite a rough start to their lives, giraffe calves start walking around one hour after birth.

• • •

Many giraffe calves are killed when they are very young by lions, leopards, hyenas and African wild dogs.

No two giraffes have the same pattern! However, calves may inherit some pattern traits from their mothers.

• • •

Giraffes only sleep 5-30 minutes per day in small bursts of 1-2 minutes.

• • •

Giraffes make many different sounds, including some that are so low-pitched humans can't hear them.

Female giraffes will often return to the place they were born to give birth to their own calves.

• • •

Giraffe tongues can be up to 20 inches (50.8 cm) long! They are also dark-colored due to melanin, which helps to provide sun protection.

• • •

Giraffes have horns covered in hair. They are called **ossicones**. They serve no purpose in females, but males often use them as a weapon in fighting.

Such big animals require a lot of food! In fact, giraffes eat over 75 lb (34 kg) of food per day — meaning they spend most of their time eating.

・・・

The scientific name for the giraffe is *Giraffa camelopardalis*. This name comes from the Ancient Greeks' belief that giraffes looked like camels wearing a leopard's coat.

・・・

Due to their elongated body shape, giraffes need powerful hearts. A giraffe's heart is around 2 feet (61 cm) in length and weighs up to 25 lbs (11.3 kg). It is the largest of any land mammal.

THE ULTIMATE GIRAFFE BOOK

A giraffe drinking water in Zambia. Can you see the birds on its back?

When male giraffes want to show dominance, they engage in an act called **necking**. This involves head-butting each other! However, it rarely ends in death — the weaker giraffe will usually just back off.

...

In general, giraffes aren't fighters. They will usually run from threats, but if necessary they will use their long and strong legs to kick a predator.

...

If a male giraffe wants to test how fertile a female giraffe is, he will taste her urine!

Since 2014, June 21 is **World Giraffe Day**. It is celebrated on the longest day of the year, to recognize their record-breaking height.

· · ·

Julius Caesar brought the first giraffe to Europe in 46 B.C. Nowadays, the only **giraffes** in Europe are in zoos.

A young giraffe.

THE ULTIMATE GIRAFFE BOOK

Sadly, giraffes are already extinct in seven countries in Africa.

• • •

Although scientists don't know for sure how long giraffes usually live, they estimate that in the wild it is approximately 25 years. Giraffes kept in captivity generally live longer, sometimes up to 40 years.

• • •

Giraffes have large, round feet — around 11.8 inches (30 cm) in diameter!

Giraffes have one-way valves in their necks to prevent too much blood from rushing to their brains when they bend down to drink water.

• • •

NASA has studied giraffes, in particular their blood vessels, to help develop new human spacesuits.

• • •

Sadly, the number of giraffes in the wild is decreasing. In the 1980s, there were approximately 150,000 wild giraffes. Now, it is around 111,000. While these numbers are Africa-wide, in some areas, they have seen a 95% drop in giraffe populations.

THE ULTIMATE GIRAFFE BOOK

A giraffe calf in Kariega Game Reserve, Grahamstown, South Africa. © Zoë Reeve

Giraffes are listed as **vulnerable** by the *International Union for Conservation of Nature*, however, individual species have different ratings.

• • •

Three subspecies of giraffes are on the endangered or critically-endangered list.

• • •

The giraffe has only one close relative: the okapi. The okapi is a rare animal, which slightly resembles a zebra.

Giraffes are **herbivores**, meaning they only eat plants. They are browsing animals, so their diet consists of leaves and buds from trees as well as flowers and fruit when available.

• • •

Giraffe eating habits are believed to contribute to pollination as they spread seeds around when they eat and after digestion.

• • •

Although they don't do it very often, when giraffes lie down they do so with their legs folded underneath their bodies.

A mother and her calf in Serengeti, Tanzania.
© *Hu Chen*

THE ULTIMATE GIRAFFE BOOK

A giraffe using its extra long tongue to grab some food.

Giraffes will usually spend more time grazing for food during the dry season, as it's much harder to find food. They are also known to graze during moonlit nights, while they rest during darker nights.

· · ·

Why do giraffes have long necks? There are several reasons, including so they can reach food that no animals other than elephants can reach, and they are able to keep a lookout over large distances for predators.

A giraffe's spots are not only for camouflage. Beneath them is a complicated blood vessel system, with each spot a 'window' for releasing excess body heat.

• • •

Giraffes live in groups, usually made up of either related females (and offspring), or unrelated males. However, their groups can change daily, and they are not territorial.

Giraffes live in scattered populations across southern and eastern sub-Saharan Africa.

• • •

Giraffes have large, bulging eyes on either side of their heads, which give them an all-around vision.

• • •

The color of the patches/spots on a giraffe's coat can be orange, chestnut, brown or nearly black. The fur in between is a white or light cream color.

Male giraffes' spots become darker as they get older. This is a good way to tell the age of a giraffe.

• • •

Giraffes use their long tongues to reach and grab foliage, as well as to groom themselves.

• • •

If there is a sandstorm or lots of insects, giraffes are able to close both their nostrils!

THE ULTIMATE GIRAFFE BOOK

A giraffe and her calf in Masai Mara Game Reserve, Kenya. © TANAKA Juuyoh

What's under their beautiful coats? Their skin color is either gray or tan. The skin is thick to prevent injuries when rummaging through thorny bushes.

• • •

Giraffes have parasite repellants in their fur, which give them a very distinctive scent.

• • •

Giraffes have 3.3 ft (1 m) long tails with a tuft of dark hair on the end, which they use to flick away insects.

A giraffe's **ossicones** (horns) can be used to tell the age and gender of the animal. Females and young giraffes have thin ossicones with a tuft of hair on top, while males usually have bald-topped ossicones. Male giraffes may also have a smaller third lump in the center of their heads.

• • •

Giraffes don't have any upper teeth.

• • •

Giraffes don't have many predators and are one of the longest living mammals in their habitat. Their biggest threat is the lion, and occasionally hyenas.

A giraffe drinking water.

THE ULTIMATE GIRAFFE BOOK

A tower of giraffes.

Giraffes are prone to parasites such as ticks. However, birds like the red-billed and yellow-billed Oxpeckers can often be found picking the parasites off of giraffes.

...

In Namibia, there is a life-size rock carving of a giraffe that dates back over 8,000 years.

...

There are many African folk tales that include the giraffe — most of which talk about how the giraffe got its long neck. For example, a tale from eastern Africa tells that the giraffe got its long neck from eating too many magic herbs.

There is a star constellation called *Camelopardalis*, which is in the shape of a giraffe. It is large but faint — so you can only see it on very dark nights.

• • •

The Rothschild's giraffe is the rarest giraffe in the world. There are only an estimated 1,669 left in the wild.

• • •

In Nairobi, Kenya is the Giraffe Manor hotel. There, you can wake up to a rare Rothschild's giraffe peeping through your window!

Oh, hey!

The giraffe is the national animal of Tanzania.

• • •

A giraffe's head can turn completely vertically, which helps it to get hard-to-reach food in the trees.

• • •

Female giraffes have a **gestation period** (the duration of the pregnancy) of 14 months.

• • •

Female giraffes are able to start breeding around 48–60 months. For males, it is around 42 months.

Completely white giraffes have been spotted in the wild, however, this is very rare and is caused by a condition called **leucism**.

• • •

Have you ever seen a giraffe walk? They move both legs on one side first, then the other side, which is quite peculiar! The camel also walks like this.

• • •

Giraffes can mate at any time during the year.

A young reticulated giraffe calf in Lewa Wildlife Conservancy, Isiolo, Kenya. © David Clode

It is very rare for a giraffe to have twins; they usually just have one calf.

• • •

Giraffe calves are born with their horns, which is rare. However, they are lying flat on their head during birth and pop up around one week later.

• • •

Female calves tend to stay within their mother's home ground for most of their lives, while male calves usually wander off on their own after three years.

Male and female giraffes have slightly different eating techniques, which reduces competition for food. Female giraffes bend down to reach lower leaves and branches, while the males reach up high into the trees looking for food.

...

Sadly, the decline in giraffe numbers is mostly due to humans, including poaching, habitat loss and agriculture that takes over land that giraffes would usually roam on.

While giraffes aren't so picky about what they eat, they do have a favorite — the acacia tree.

• • •

A group of giraffes is called a **tower**.

• • •

Giraffes can be described as **even-toed ungulates**. This means that they are hoofed animals that carry their weight evenly on an even number of their toes. There are around 270 land animals in this category, including camels, antelopes, alpacas and goats.

Giraffes can weigh more than a car — up to 2 tons (1900 kg)!

• • •

Despite being a symbol of Africa, giraffes are believed to have originally been from the cooler parts of Eurasia around 7-8 million years ago.

• • •

A giraffe's large, round hooves provide greater surface area to stop them from sinking into the sand despite their heavy weight.

Until a few years ago, scientists believed that giraffes were the only mammal that couldn't swim. However, in 2010 a study showed that giraffes probably can swim, they just choose not to!

・・・

Giraffes have a cooling system in their noses, which helps to keep their brains 34.4 °F (3 °C) lower than the rest of the body.

・・・

When giraffes are hot, they don't sweat or pant. This is one of the reasons why they don't need to drink so much water.

The famous toy shop *Toys 'R' Us* chose a giraffe as their first mascot in the 1950s. His name was *Geoffrey the Giraffe*.

• • •

Giraffes have the longest tail of all mammals.

• • •

Giraffe mothers will often team up and babysit each other's calves while they are out hunting for food.

• • •

A giraffe's tongue is **prehensile**. This means that they can use it to grab things, just like a hand.

As well as amazing tongues, giraffe mouths are covered in hard, finger-like papillae to protect them from thorny plants and bushes.

• • •

When a giraffe takes a step, it's about 15 feet (4.6 m) in length!

• • •

A newborn calf weighs around 220 lb (100 kg).

• • •

A giraffe's blood pressure is twice that of a human. They need it to get blood all the way up their long necks!

Giraffes have 32 teeth, all on the bottom jaw.

• • •

Giraffes use their bottom row of teeth to comb leaves off of trees.

• • •

Giraffes' tongues are so long that they can clean their ears with them!

• • •

If you ever get the chance to meet a giraffe, remember that they hate having their heads touched!

Although giraffes only eat plants, they are often seen licking and chewing on animal bones. This is to get more calcium into their bodies than they can get from plants.

• • •

Calves drink milk from their mothers for 4–6 months. While they will have a taste of leaves before then, it's not until seven months old that their mother helps them fully transition into their new diet.

• • •

Giraffes are the third-heaviest animals in the world, after elephants and rhinos.

The West African giraffe almost became extinct in the 1990s. There were only 50 left in the wild, but after quick action from conservationists, they brought the number up to 450.

・・・

There are many ways to help conserve giraffes in the wild. There are lots of organizations and government programs, such as *Giraffe Conservation Alliance, The Giraffe Conservation Foundation* and the *African Fund for Endangered Wildlife*. You can check out their websites to find out ways that you can help giraffes!

THE ULTIMATE GIRAFFE BOOK

1. How many species of giraffe are there?

2. Where do giraffes live?

3. What is one of the giraffe's favorite foods?

4. Which is the rarest type of giraffe?

5. What is the closest living relative to the giraffe?

A mother and her calf. © Hein waschefort

THE ULTIMATE GIRAFFE BOOK

6   How does a giraffe drink water?

7   For how long does a calf drink its mother's milk?

8   How many teeth do giraffes have?

9   How much does a newborn calf weigh?

10 Can you remember the scientific name for a giraffe?

11 What are the horns on the top of a giraffe's head called?

12 What is a male giraffe called?

13 What do you call a group of giraffes?

14 Can giraffes swim?

15 Giraffes often have twins. True or false?

16 The giraffe is the national animal of which African country?

17 What type of bird that can often be seen hitching a ride on a giraffe?

18 Male giraffe spots get lighter as they get older. True or false?

19 What is it called when giraffes fight each other?

20 How many toes does a giraffe have?

THE ULTIMATE GIRAFFE BOOK

Two male giraffes necking at San Francisco Zoo. © *Brocken Inaglory*

ANSWERS

1. Four.

2. Sub-Saharan Africa.

3. Acacia tree.

4. The Rothschild's giraffe.

5. The okapi.

6. It spreads its legs so it can reach down to the water.

7. 4-6 months.

8. 32.

9. Around 220 lb (100 kg).

10. Camelopardalis.

11. Ossicones.

12. A bull.

13. A tower.

14. Technically, yes. But no one has ever seen it!

15. False. Twins are very rare.

16. Tanzania.

17. Oxpecker.

18. False. They get darker.

19. Necking.

20. Two.

GIRAFFE
WORD SEARCH

A	D	R	O	T	H	S	C	H	I	L	D
P	G	B	A	V	Z	S	D	F	E	S	H
O	A	I	F	B	A	A	V	C	X	A	I
T	E	R	R	C	E	C	M	N	B	V	U
Q	T	G	I	A	W	A	A	D	S	A	T
S	E	F	C	Q	F	L	V	C	V	N	D
D	V	D	A	Z	S	F	Z	Y	I	N	H
F	C	S	A	Q	V	C	E	G	F	A	R
V	Z	O	S	S	I	C	O	N	E	H	N
T	O	W	E	R	U	Y	T	E	G	D	F
M	M	N	C	R	Q	W	Z	D	F	G	S
N	S	F	R	N	E	C	K	I	N	G	K

Can you find all the words below in the word search puzzle on the left?

GIRAFFE	SAVANNAH	OSSICONE
CALF	NECKING	ROTHSCHILD
TOWER	AFRICA	ACACIA

THE ULTIMATE GIRAFFE BOOK

SOLUTION

			R	O	T	H	S	C	H	I	L	D
		G		A							S	
			I	F		A					A	
			R			C					V	
			I	A		A	A				A	
			C		F	L		C			N	
			A			F			I		N	
							E				A	
			O	S	S	I	C	O	N	E	H	
T	O	W	E	R								
				N	E	C	K	I	N	G		

SOURCES

"11 Facts About Giraffes". 2020. *Dosomething. Org.* https://www.dosomething.org/us/facts/11-facts-about-giraffes.

National Geographic Society. *"Giraffe." Accessed October 21, 2022.*

Gammon, Crystal. *"Fun Facts About Giraffes."* **LiveScience.** *Accessed October 21, 2022.*

"20 Things You Might Not Know About Giraffes". **2014. Mentalfloss.Com.** *https://www.mentalfloss.com/article/56318/20-things-you-might-not-know-about-giraffes.*

"13 Fascinating Giraffe Facts - Giraffe Conservation Foundation". 2020. Giraffe Conservation Foundation. *https://giraffeconservation.org/facts/13-fascinating-giraffe-facts/.*

Fennessy, Julian; Bidon, Tobias; Reuss, Friederike; Kumar, Vikas; Elkan, Paul; Nilsson, Maria A.; Vamberger, Melita; Fritz, Uwe; Janke, Axel (2016). *"Multi-locus Analyses reveal four giraffe species instead of one".* Current Biology. 26 (18): 2543–2549. doi:10.1016/j.cub.2016.07.036. PMID 27618261. S2CID 3991170

Greaves, N.; Clement, R. (2000). *When Hippo Was Hairy: And Other Tales from Africa.* Struik. pp. 86–88. ISBN 978-1-86872-456-7.

"Giraffe". Online Etymology Dictionary. *Retrieved 7 October 2022.*

"Rothschild's Giraffe". 2020. En.Wikipedia.Org. *https://en.wikipedia.org/wiki/Rothschild%27s_giraffe.*

"Giraffe". 2020. Young People's Trust For The Environment. *https://ypte.org.uk/factsheets/giraffe/conservation.*

"10 Giraffe Facts! | National Geographic Kids". 2016. National Geographic Kids. *https://www.natgeokids.com/uk/discover/animals/general-animals/ten-giraffe-facts/.*

2020. Yorkshirewildlifepark.Com. *https://www.yorkshirewildlifepark.com/9-unusual-facts-giraffes-may-astound/.*

Lifeforms, Animals, and 40 Facts. 2018. "40 Unusual Giraffe Facts - Serious Facts". Serious Facts. *https://www.seriousfacts.com/giraffe-facts/.*

"17 Fun Facts About Giraffes (Some Are Hilariously Unbelievable)". 2019. Africa Freak. *https://africafreak.com/fun-facts-about-giraffes.*

We hope you learned some awesome facts about giraffes! We'd love it if you left us a **review**—it always makes us smile :) And more importantly, reviews help other readers make better buying decisions.

Visit us at **www.bellanovabooks.com** for the latest books.

ALSO BY JENNY KELLETT

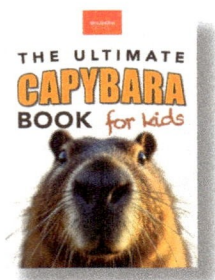  

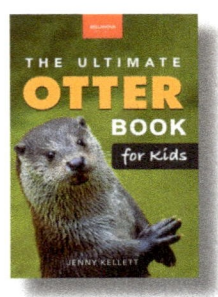 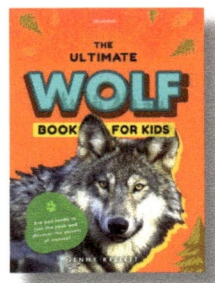 

... and more!

Available at

www.bellanovabooks.com

and all major online bookstores.

www.ingramcontent.com/pod-product-compliance
Lightning Source LLC
LaVergne TN
LVHW050134080526
838202LV00061B/6485